𝕲𝖗𝖆𝖞𝖘𝖔𝖓

SELECTED WORK
2003–2020

Dear Cassie and Chris,

I hope you have a wonderful
life together!

[signature] 2021

Copyright

I dedicate this collection to departed friends
and family members who live on in my heart:

Natascha Grayson
Leslie Stonehold
Ryan Pearce
Linda Swinburn
Hannah McAllister
Bruce Curtayne
Joanne Fagon
Alexander Thynn

"Not even death will kill them."

With thanks to Maria Amaya for the cover illustration, Kieron Edwards for the internal illustrations, and Libby Sidebotham for the design and typography.
Also with special gratitude to my wife Caz, for pushing me to collate this work, my dad Nigel, for helping to turn this book into a reality, my mum Jayne, for sparking my interest in storytelling, and to Emma Manners, the Duchess of Rutland, for her faith and patronage.

CONTENTS

PART I

Early Years

2003–2007

PART II

Decadent Romanticism

2008–2013

PART III

A Poet-In-Residence

2014–2020

PART I

—

Early Years
2003–2007

Trance of the Sceptical Sailor

Inspired by 'The Siren', John William Waterhouse

"Harp song on a Siren's breeze
will trap the flotsam mind",
(Legends told on raging seas
Are letters to the blind).

"Living art by ragged coast,
This mistress of Neptune
Glimmers like a gorgeous ghost
And shimmers with the moon".

Slender fingers stroked a string
And whispers licked the gloom,
Crowned with spray, the sailor king
Floundered towards his doom.

Red soles ripped on rusted rocks
And staggered with the shore,
Dazed eyes twitched like broken clocks
As sea-salt stung the sore.

Sharp claws scratched the captain's skin;
I mouthed a silent prayer.
Rags in ears, I turned to sin
And left him screaming there.

Some sailors will not listen
To tales from this 'old crone',
Until they hear a kissing
Of Harpy's teeth – on bone.

Infernal Madici

A journey through madness

I. Introduction

A squirming city under streets of Rome
stretches skin over this organ tome
for the drummer to beat this drum
of lies and vice, traitors and spies

and when forsaken travellers pass through
the rotting gates on their journey to
the eternal burn, some remain,
flickering shadows of a dying flame.

So now, my friends, 'tis time we begin
this glorious story of glorious sin.
Watch fiery rust rip autumn leaves
and spread like cancer through sleeping trees.

II. Orchestra

Manacle Smiles

Frantic for freedom, hot echoes harpoon
from the reign of revolt to the cold.
Now the puppets of kings reattach shackle strings
for a contract of glittering gold.

The Bazaar

Nobody but naivety listens
to pleading notes of the mute,
a coin is spent in the beggar's tin
as gratitude feathers the flute.

His playful notes of love speak truth
but notes of truth hide lies,
and buried in this lying tune
are notes of his demise.

The music stops. Nobody sees
the beggar become the dead,
for no artist makes a profit
from painting the landscape red.

III. Revolution Prophesied

It trudges through ornate debris,
this one-eyed creature (not born of Eve)
and on its back it grows a tree
with arms for branches, balloons for leaves

and in these leaves it harvests light
and beauty from the world above
to display as bad, despite
the shining goodness, shining love,

but a two-eyed warrior will appear
in the skin of a one-eyed fiend,
crouching in his hand: a spear,
and in his mind: a guillotine.

This champion will charm the beast's balloons
with rockfall whispers, a sharpened kiss,
branches will fall from a righteous wound
and truth will light the necropolis.

IV. Shadows through the Smoke

Synthetic Eye

No words that I've written can be left unread,
no secret memories can be left unsaid,
my mind is Tourette's with two seconds delay,
no vines at my waist will constrict my say.
They grip and they bite, they scratch and they chafe,
they try to restrict me from keeping them safe,
but I can't let myself blink, for I know I will miss
a punch, a theft, a step, a kiss.

Truth Changes

A riptide of hate infects the pages
and false truths move through empty cages.
Knowledge: removed by a faceless thief
(one smile will distort broken seconds of grief).

The Chef's Special

Chain-gang children shuffle their feet,
twitching to the rhythm of the advert beat.
They wait for the scraps down Restaurant Street,
then sneak to the Pale Chef's private suite
(where sweeteners pickle in clear deceit)
yet their harlequin smiles still continue to eat!

V. Finale

Awakened by an emerald
(in the muddy wash)

This anarchic verse will mark
the decline of the Pale Chef's control,
a scar on the face of the creature,
a fire without timber or coal.

I. *Discovery*
Wading through the muddy wash,
Suspicion discovers a leaf.
Wisdom removes the mask of truth
and startles the faceless thief.

II. *Disbelief*
Frozen lids crack open,
young pupils find the lies,
chapped mouths now bleed with rumours, but
their careless talk costs lives.

III. *Denial*
Shutting their eyes, they burn the books
of truth and brand them Sophistry.
"This verse", they spit from haunted lips,
"is treason dressed as prophecy."

IV. *Destruction*
Curiosity endures the ascent,
forcing open the gates with his youth,
but the small trickle becomes a torrent
and Madici drowns in the truth.

V.
The fugitive surfaces from this tomb of midnight blue, and emerges
into darkness. His distressed body cries with remnants of the life
he left behind. Staggering forward, he drops to his knees, his eyes
adjusting to the gradually expanding world.

Void

Cool mist swirls around his ankles as he walks briskly
in the pale morning light.
His vision is fixed on nothing and everything – indistinguishable
points in the distance, the dull colours of the new dawn,
a stranger wearing familiar faces.
Usually a deep thinker, he surprises himself by his lack of creativity;
the ideas he manages to capture trickle through his mind like
water through a sieve.
Nothing matters to him anymore.
The silence fails to play a melody to the chords of his breaking
heart, for (he convinces himself) what was once a feeling
is now nothing but a memory.
Maybe it was nothing.
Maybe it was everything.
Half way across a bridge he stops to watch the magnificence
of the sunrise.
His mind wanders somewhere else.

Arrival

Above the stars, in lands of bliss,
angelic wisps of Genesis
slip over floating dunes of dreams
to pick horizons at their seams.

Like dandelions in windswept trance,
their coils of daring freedom dance
into the cracks of new-born light
where Mania laughs in sane delight.

Once more, anarchic verses shift
through ready minds, and cast adrift
all thoughts of danger, trading pain
for sung delirium, whirlwind flame.

So follow me into the land
of Liberty, is it not something grand
to live a life without a care?
But wait! Here the pages tear...

PART II

Decadent Romanticism
2008–2013

The Poetry Brothel

Come artists and poets, ascend to the throne
of looking-glass paper, your face is unknown!
Do you paint for the daydreams of clowns, or of kings?
Do you long to breathe life into dusty writings?
Then whore out your work! They'll pay by the page
(for a little bit lower than minimum wage)
at the Poetry Brothel, that scandalous den:
give voice to the vices of Monsters and Men!

The Restoration of Babylon

I drank, and felt the darkness flood
into my mouth; I tasted blood
as I trod on through ash and mud
to gaze upon the wall.
The words that once bled ancient doom
still pierced the veil of choking gloom
which crept, like mist, throughout the room
of Belshazzar's great ball.
Before the Babel wine was sipped
our Lord did make this feast a crypt;
his mocking otherworldly script
still read "All empires fall."
And to this wall, I took my pen,
and scored a plea for better men:
"Great empires will still rise again
if great minds raise the call."

Confronting Death

(An Inevitability)

In Memoriam H.M.

> A turbulent flash and the night was aflame,
> a young star blazed greatly, then faded again.
> Shock leant me a tear, I mumbled a prayer,
> the darkness, engulfing the light of her flair
> wept gold-dust. Her glow was now shimmering rain,
> a shining reminder: love conquers despair.

The Outstretched Hand

> I've heard there is an outstretched hand
> near where the breath of life departs
> which takes you to the ancient land
> of beauty (where all beauty starts),
> and though you cannot see it now
> (your march has not nearly begun)
> one day, she'll reach and show you how
> eyes close – and open to the sun.

The Redemption of Judas

Inspired by the Gospel of Judas

Ten Hell-hounds charge through blood and flame,
in tow, the blazing chariot
of He whose curse became His name,
that wretch, Judas Iscariot.

Black oceans burst, erupting light,
and this dark soul is draggéd hence,
His hounds grow wings of Godly might
to fight the winds of Man's pretence

And charge! They charge through burning clouds
and snake as eels through molten skies
to save this wretch from Satan's crowds
and free His name from ancient lies.

Now lightning strikes and thunder rolls,
His hounds are whipped with icy rain
but push, they push – towards their goal,
and pant, they pant – in holy pain.

They see the gates! There, Jesus grins,
they quickly stop, but Judas stays:
"I have no strength for all these sins,
when all I did, Lord, was obey."

"The fire's yet to take its toll…"
purrs Jesus to burnt chariot,
and lays His kiss on that poor soul,
that Saint, Judas Iscariot.

The Opium Den

Milk-white smoke was suckled from the oak of Avalon
which gnarled at our pomposity 'til all respect had gone.
We looked to heaven's entrants from our thrones of thistle-mead
and judged our masters' writings like gaunt saplings to the seed.

They whirled us like a Dervish up to unexpected heights,
we saw Death, like an arrow, cut poor dreamers down mid-flight;
we sipped a liquor tourniquet, a pleasure-dome forlorn,
and slipped into a kingdom from whence radicals were born.

Our screams for revolution reached the Sacrificial Spire,
but we had licked the nectar Death had held in heaven's fire,
and as we fell with broken wings down from the blinding sky
to drown in pools of drug-laced tears, we heard no mourners cry.

Confessions of a Lotus Eater

Worthy and wicked, I found myself faced
with a summit of sin: a cathedral debased.
A veiled woman, guarding the door with a stare
had sensed me, and I her, in that frozen air.
I approached in a desolate, desperate haste
and dropped to my knees as I met with her glare.

I will try to describe how my virtues were sold
but her beauty will, somehow, still tarry untold:
black lashes of passion held beckoning eyes
concealing flecks licked with the light of fireflies
a flutter ensnared me, devotion took hold,
enraptured by hellfire in heaven's disguise.

Descending to dizzying depths, I awoke,
Head rattling with vipers, lungs laden with smoke.
The harlot was sleeping, her grail of whisky
was perched like a vulture, revolted by me.
I crept to the coldness of night's bitter cloak,
escaping the embers of raw purgatory.

Lust

I plucked the bright, sweet scented rose
whose perfume clawed inside my head,
but now her petals decompose
as they rest, scattered on my bed.

My Martyred Member

A Graysonic satire

Diseased and bloated, pompous, sick,
a limp and syphilitic prick
now weeps between two limbs of flesh
and pines for pussy. Fresh
into town they used to come,
the taxis brought them one by one,
each slut and virgin, whore and nun
was tempted by it – every one!
And who could blame them? In its prime
the cock of Leicester's walk was mine,
and its sole target, given time,
was hymens, hearts and fragile minds,
but now? All scaly, gnarled and bent,
I fear not even crack could tempt
the walkers of night's starry tent
to touch what came (and never went)
from its heroic shaft,
so if warts are medals of excess
then raise a glass to my success!
And leave me with the loneliness
of hymens, minds and hearts.

Correspondence

Commissioned by H.K.

With more than miles between us,
more than oceans, bricks or bars,
we share one vast and silent sky
and multitudes of stars,

and when we cannot see their cool
and faint light fill the air,
we still know that they're burning –
you still know that I'm there.

And we may never get to do
the things friend's often do,
but we can write and share our souls,
and black skies can turn blue.

The Order of Chivalry

In this great age of turbulence,
there is a goal for which we strive
and when we see a thing in need,
the order is to stay alive –

but at what cost, another's health?
Would we forsake our honour thus?
Does death breed fear, or fear bring death
if life's last hope depends on us?

Yet, words are cold. Such icy winds
have whipped from many mouths before,
but not this day. Today we know
such hollow vows will reign no more,

and live or die, our legacy
will slowly move from town to field
'til one day, folk may think of us
when they decide to raise their shield.

The Infamous Nomadica

for Her Majesty Queen Elizabeth II

Pray, Ladies and Gentlemen, do not be afraid
Of this haggard complexion, half covered in shade,
Half covered in trinkets, gold piercings and bands,
I'm no common gypsy or seller of sands,
I'm English, once captured by slaver crusade
And sold to a nomad of far stranger lands.

My story shall start in the midst of a dream,
When awoken, was I, by this most ghastly scene:
White wolves of the waste were attacking my wife,
Red dress ripped and tattered, eyes vacant of life,
Blood stains on her fingers, mouth frozen mid-scream,
Her body a scabbard, my merciful knife.

And so my eyes opened, but not to this act,
I was staring up, skywards, from blind Samél's back,
My sweat-rags were soaking, my lips could not part,
My dream kept repeating, dark rocks in my heart,
Then Samél, the nomad, made my bindings slack
And I hit the floor as he turned to depart.

"Young English", he said in an accent unknown,
"I'll point you the way to which you can go home.
Head westwards through forests and cities of night,
And ask at the village of Mountain Moonlight.
If no-one will help you, just show them this stone"
And held out a crystal as white as starlight.

"That crystal, she comes from a land in the sea
Which you have the honour to call your country,
She was torn from your ground by the rich and the free
Turned into a nomad; poor nomad like me.
So English, I beg you, hear this wretched plea,
And take her back home, patriot refugee."

Samél vanished into a flourish of heat
Which lapped from a distance like waves at his feet.
I drank 'til the flagon he'd left me ran dry,
Then started my journey to blue westward sky,
Not caring what wondrous new creatures I'd meet,
Just wanting to hear my wife's sweet lullaby.

My wife, my beloved, my soul's second half:
Britannia my sceptre, Britannia my staff,
Britannia my boots for this rugged terrain,
Britannia my shelter, Britannia my rain,
Britannia my teardrops, Britannia my laugh,
Britannia my freedom, Britannia my chain.

PART III

A Poet-In-Residence
2014–2020

'When all is dead but death itself,
the stubborn wind shall blow
and echoes of such fragile things
will stir the dust below.'

Todos Caeran
(All Will Fall)

For Emma Manners, Duchess of Rutland

The earth revolves on just one truth,
a force which binds us all –
that broken beings, buildings too,
are all fated to fall.

All this will turn to dust, my friends,
please heed this poet's call,
and when the dust has settled,
there shall be none left at all –

no leaves to dance in autumn's waltz
or laughter through the hall.
The mighty oaks of ancient root
know that, they too, will fall.

This earthly truth, none can control,
as none can tame the skies –
but even though the sun may fall,
the sun again shall rise,

and with the rising sun, my friends,
(hear these impassioned cries!)
we should take note that in this life
not all that's fallen dies.

A castle can be built again,
a mended wing can fly,
an acorn from a dying tree
can grow to scrape the sky,

and I'll not live this life in fear
that yes, I too, shall fall;
I'd rather fall and taste the earth
than never rise at all.

'La Gargamelle'

I heard the pallid moon was bright,
but I could not see her that night,
for I was swallowed, out of sight,
into La Gargamelle.

A chair found me, I took my place,
looked up, and saw the glowing face
of she who'd tempt the Gods from grace,
her name? La Gargamelle.

Ancient bottles, absinthe spoons,
bright candles burning back the gloom;
the paintings breathed inside that room,
they whispered: "Gargamelle".

Before my lips could utter "no",
a chalice brimming with Bordeaux
was thrust upon my table throw
to stir La Gargamelle,

and every time I took a sip,
I felt my inner poet rip
apart the chains that bound my lips
to free La Gargamelle,

and now it has escaped, I see
a world of opportunity.
In mirrors, staring back at me:
the face of Gargamelle.

Leicester's Dream

*Commissioned on behalf of Leicester City Football Club
by BBC Radio Leicester*

Back when the foxes took the lead,
they doubted and they mocked us –
"Enjoy one night of dreaming, lads,
this night is for the foxes."

We thought that this was all it was:
a dream or a delusion,
"One day", we heard the pundits say,
"they'll shatter this illusion",

but Ranieri had our backs,
"Our fans", he said, "they must dream –
the role of dreaming's for the fans
and winning's for their team."

"And we", he said, "must remain calm;
our feet, they must stay grounded",
but in each match, their feet would fly
until each whistle sounded,

and when each whistle sounded
the whole city would exhale
and erupt with such elation
that we smashed the Richter scale,

and the pundits kept on saying
that the city's bound to fail
but then Sunday after Sunday,
we would see our team prevail.

This is more than just good football,
this is more than just a sport,
for the feeling in this city
can't be bottled, can't be bought,

and so now we stand together
as one city and one team
and go straight towards that title –
all connected in one dream,

and if the foxes finish first,
remember how they mocked us –
but dreams are there for living, lads,
and winning's for the foxes.

The Tyranny of the Majority

The world is so much darker, now
our heads are in the sack.
We hear the jeering crowds, and fear
there is no turning back.

Our hands are tied, our minds are numb,
our feet keep shuffling on,
and we must fumble forwards now
the light we had has gone.

Some of us may kneel and pray,
some stand and blindly fight,
some of us may hold our tongues,
some may forget the light,

but we must fumble forwards friends,
we must show that we care,
we must defend our fellow man
when no-one else is there,

and though the crowds may taunt us
as we start this long, cold night,
remember: while there's more of them,
it doesn't mean they're right.

The Nightmare of Newstead Abbey

I could not catch a moment's sleep
so drifted through the poet's grounds
and there, I heard a maiden's weep
disturb the pool of nightly sounds,
and so I pushed into the Shade
(that starless black beneath the leaves)
and spied the pond where dreams are made
and nightmares born on Hallow's Eve,
but I was mindless of the date
and thought there would be nought to fear;
I knew the hour was drawing late,
but not that Fate was drawing near.
She waded slowly, through the night
and wept beneath the willow trees,
a marble beauty, shining bright
with stagnant matter to her knees.
My interest in this puzzle grew,
and so I asked her why she cried,
"My dear", said she, "I weep for you,
who slipped into these depths – and died."
This frightened me, and so I fled
to find my cottage through the Shade,
believing that, once tucked in bed,
the dawn would find me unafraid,
but I had left the key inside,
and I had closed the crooked door;
I feared, no matter how I tried,
that way was barred for evermore.
I peered in, through the windowpane
and saw a slowly breathing bed.

Right there, where I alone had lain
a second 'Me' now slept instead.

And to this night, I watch and pray
that soon, that 'Me' will hear Her weep,
and leave the cottage for the Shade,
and slip away, so I can sleep.

The Dreaming
(A Lullaby)

"Stay with me, my sunshine,
it will all be over soon.
Let's play among the feather clouds
before I meet the moon.

Let's drink tea with the teddy bears,
let's share their picnic spread,
then find a spot beneath the trees
for me to rest my head,

and when I have to close my eyes,
before you start to weep,
know that I'll live inside your heart:
I'll waken when you sleep,

and there, we can forever play,
we'll cuddle, read and sing.
Not even death will kill me, dear,
it's just a little thing."

Three Graces

For Violet, Alice and Eliza Manners

There was a time when girls were taught
their duty was to be a wife,
and if the Gods had graced them, they
would each be blessed throughout their life

and now, I look around and see
each grace still lifted, like a prize
to crown the head of every girl
who would believe these Classic lies.

Beauty, Charm and Joy, I spy
in all the pictures I am shown,
but airbrushed hips and painted lips
conceal the strength their subjects own.

Yes, Beauty can still play its part,
but what is Beauty to the blind?
And what, once youth and Beauty fade,
if there's no Beauty in her mind?

And Joy! We all seek happiness
and hope our girls will find it, too,
but true Joy comes from Liberty
and choosing what they want to do,

and in their hearts, they'll know what's right
with strength to rival any man's;
and none will damage their resolve
to Honour their own righteous plans,

and when they leave a legacy
of triumphs modest and profound,
their Charm will be Humility:
their feet still rooted to the ground.

So let's discard that man-made crown
our girls still shape their heads to wear;
and celebrate three graces that
can fit o'er every infant's hair,

for if they Honour what is true
to who they are and what they feel
they'll always have the Liberty
to Humbly pursue what is real
(and not those lies of Classic men
who saw young girls as works of art).

There's none more graceful than the child
who knows her mind and trusts her heart.

Lament For Icarus
(Introduction and Melody)

Allegro ♩ = 160

'Portrait of a Brothellian Poet'
Kieron Edwards, 2010.

About the Author

Tim Grayson (born 1987) is a poet and creative polymath
with a range of experience in multiple fields, including
art, literature, politics, technology, media, philosophy,
music, philanthropy and physical culture.

His work and projects have taken him all over the globe.

Tim is also a lifelong martial artist, with a particular
interest in submission grappling, fencing (sabre) and
traditional ('Golden Age') training methods.

He lives in Leicester (UK) with his wife and two children.

worksofgrayson.com